COLONIAL VIRGINIA

A PICTURE BOOK TO REMEMBER HER BY

Designed by
DAVID GIBBON

Produced by
TED SMART

CRESCENT

INTRODUCTION

Virginia has one of the longest continuous histories of any American state, dating from 1607 when pioneer settlers arrived from England and landed at the site of present-day Jamestown. They named this part of the New World after Elizabeth I, the "Virgin Queen", and it was an area which, under the original charter, included lands west of the Atlantic seaboard settlements, to the Mississippi River and beyond.

Those early pioneers, representatives of the Virginia Company, intended not only to colonize, but to open up new areas for trade, introduce Christianity and prevent the Spanish from occupying more land in the vast continent. The conditions they encountered were more harsh than they could ever have imagined for not only did their supplies, brought in their tiny ships, Discovery, Constant and Godspeed, quickly run out, but they also met with fierce hostility from local Red Indian tribes who were enraged by their intrusion, and their numbers were drastically reduced by disease.

To their aid came another Englishman, John Rolfe, who was married to Pocahontas, a Red Indian princess. He realised the potential of a plant grown locally by the Indians, called tobacco, which grew virtually like a weed and the leaves of which the Indians smoked. There was a rapidly expanding market for this commodity in Europe, a market that even today is still vital to Virginia's economy. Tobacco plantations were soon established along the coast, near creeks or river mouths, where the trading ships could easily moor to load and unload their cargoes.

In 1619 Africans were first brought to Jamestown as indentured servants and it was not until several decades later that they became slaves. Their role in the plantation system was of paramount importance and without them the state of Virginia would not have been so prosperous. At the start of the Civil War they accounted for approximately half the population.

Britain's first royal colony was founded in 1624 when the Virginia Company's charter was revoked, yet the first seeds of democracy had already been sown five years earlier when the first Virginia Assembly had met at Jamestown. Although the English Government strove to govern fully, their American colonies were not allowed the full rights of Englishmen in their homeland, and a growing restlessness for self-government increased. From this restlessness such men as George Washington, Thomas Jefferson, Patrick Henry and George Mason emerged as leaders in the period that led to the American Revolution, a war that resulted in independence for the American colonies.

The first shots of war were fired at Lexington, Massachusetts in April 1775, where British troops, sent to seize illegal military stores, were attacked by the local militia and the ensuing skirmish at Concord, followed by the important victory at the Battle of Bunker Hill in June, lent considerable encouragement to the American dream of independence.

Soon after, George Washington returned to arms and took command of what was then a largely ill-armed and poorly disciplined force. In March 1776, however, he successfully routed the British from Boston and on the 4th July the Continental Congress issued the Declaration of Independence. Thomas Jefferson was the principal author of this important document which renounced all allegiance to the British Crown and so severed the political connection.

The climactic battle of Yorktown, in 1781, resulted in the defeat of the British forces led by General Cornwallis, and after the fall of other southern ports only New York remained in British hands. Peace negotiations commenced in 1782 and finally, on the 3rd September 1783, the Treaty of Paris recognized American Independence.

By 1778 Virginia had abolished the African slave trade, but slavery continued to support the state's agricultural policy. In 1861 Virginia followed its neighbours in seceding from the Union it had helped to form, and Jefferson Davis was appointed the President of the Confederate States throughout the duration of the Civil War.

The Union troops were led by Abraham Lincoln and much of the fighting took place on Virginian soil, particularly around Richmond, the Confederate capital. Fierce battles were also fought at Manassas, Petersburg and Fredericksburg, the latter a regular target, being positioned between Richmond and the warring capital of Washington.

When, in April 1865, General Robert E. Lee, commander of the army of North Virginia, surrendered to the Federal General, Ulysses S. Grant, at the Appomatox Court House, Davis attempted to continue the struggle until his capture at Irwinville and subsequent imprisonment. The war was at an end, and three years later Grant was elected the 18th President of the United States of America.

The Civil War left Virginia devastated and deeply in debt and although the State was readmitted to the Union in 1870 real recovery did not begin until after World War I. Only when Harry F. Byrd Sr. became governor, in 1926, did agricultural and industrial development strengthen. The economy was also augmented by the numerous military installations established both during and after World War II, and today the State benefits from her proximity to Washington D.C., with its important research centres.

Virginia's pleasing climate and beautiful scenery attract countless visitors every year. For the adventure lover there is hiking along the Appalachian Trail, sailing on the Chesapeake River, canoeing on the Shenandoah, or skiing in the Blue Ridge Mountains. Golf courses in their picturesque settings abound, and swimming, surfing and fishing are popular activities along the Atlantic Coast. The State Parks and National Forests provide spectacular views and many of the old tobacco plantations continue to thrive, carrying on the great traditions of those early and courageous settlers.

Historically the State is exceptionally fascinating, with the triangle of Jamestown, Williamsburg and Yorktown containing a wealth of exquisitely restored buildings of the 18th century; George Washington's famous house and estate, Mount Vernon near Alexandria, and Monticello, the home that Thomas Jefferson designed himself, whilst at Jamestown are the full-size reproductions of those first tiny vessels that landed in 1607 and were to have so much influence on the future of this American State.

Williamsburg's authentic restoration project is evidenced by its picturesque houses *left, below and overleaf* and working windmill *above,* while the Governor's Palace *right* served as both home and office for several royal governors under the British Crown.

Forming the capital of the colony of Virginia between 1699 and 1799, Williamsburg was named in honour of William III. Beautifully restored to preserve its 18th century appearance, its numerous houses, shops and buildings *these pages*, set amid tranquil greenery, have been reconstructed on their original foundations. Recreating this colourful period of American history, the preservation project, begun in 1926 by the efforts of the Reverend W.A.R. Goodwin and John D. Rockefeller Jr., is administered by The Colonial Williamsburg Foundation, which also provides cultural and educational programmes.

Throughout the seasons visitors to Williamsburg can enjoy the presentations of the colourfully costumed Colonial Williamsburg militia company illustrated *on these pages.* Displays by the company include drilling, special salutes, to the accompaniment of fifes and drums, and tactical demonstrations of the muskets and cannons which were used by the valiant troops who fought so desperately on Virginia soil to win their independence from the British Crown during the war-torn years of the Revolution. The majority of these particularly exciting musters take place in the Market Square and are amongst the most popular attractions of this Historic Area.

In the 18th century Williamsburg was a small, flourishing craft centre where master craftsmen, journeymen and apprentices fashioned jewellery, clocks and musical instruments and worked as coopers, basketmakers, housewrights or cabinetmakers. Today one of the most fascinating aspects of the old town is to see the revival of these old skills, as men and women in period costume recreate the traditional methods in a score of busy, cluttered and often noisy shops. With skill and resourcefulness, the hooper *above left*, baker *centre left and below*, bootmakers *above and above right*, cabinetmaker *below left* and basket weaver *below right*, reveal the techniques used by a vital section of the colonial population.

The milliner *above* deftly completes one of the wide-brimmed bonnets worn by fashionable young ladies in the 18th century, while *left and below* can be seen the spinning and weaving, which, like candle making *right*, was usually carried out in the home by the women of the family.

Once the glittering centre of the colony's social and political life before the Revolution, the Governor's Palace *above* is Williamsburg's most elegant and imposing building. The ballroom *below* is contained in a wing which is believed to have been added in 1751 when the interior was remodelled, whilst *left* is shown part of the Palace kitchen.

Although not a part of the Historic Area, Merchant's Square *above right* has been designed in 18th and 19th century styles and is a picturesque business and shopping district.

The lovely Coke-Garret House on Nicholson Street is pictured *right*.

SHIRLEY

THE HOUSE IS A SHORT DISTANCE SOUTH. SHIRLEY WAS FIRST OCCUPIED IN 1613 AND WAS KNOWN AS WEST-AND-SHIRLEY HUNDRED. IN 1664, EDWARD HILL PATENTED THE PLACE, WHICH WAS LEFT BY THE THIRD EDWARD HILL TO HIS SISTER, ELIZABETH CARTER, IN 1720. HERE WAS BORN ANNE HILL CARTER, MOTHER OF ROBERT E. LEE, WHO OFTEN VISITED SHIRLEY. THE PRESENT HOUSE WAS BUILT ABOUT 1740.

GREENWAY

THIS WAS THE HOME OF JOHN TYLER, GOVERNOR OF VIRGINIA, 1808-1811. HIS SON, JOHN TYLER, PRESIDENT OF THE UNITED STATES, WAS BORN HERE, MARCH 29, 1790.

Historical signs *this page* provide brief records of some of the finest plantation houses, such as Greenway *centre right,* which were once the homes of patriots, presidents and others who set their mark on the country's history. The estates, many of which have remained in the same families over successive generations, are meticulously tended and still provide income from their crops.

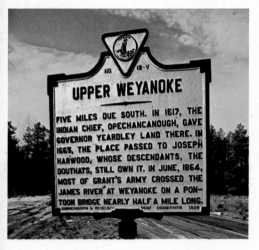

UPPER WEYANOKE

FIVE MILES DUE SOUTH. IN 1617, THE INDIAN CHIEF, OPECHANCANOUGH, GAVE GOVERNOR YEARDLEY LAND THERE. IN 1665, THE PLACE PASSED TO JOSEPH HARWOOD, WHOSE DESCENDANTS, THE DOUTHATS, STILL OWN IT. IN JUNE, 1864, MOST OF GRANT'S ARMY CROSSED THE JAMES RIVER AT WEYANOKE ON A PONTOON BRIDGE NEARLY HALF A MILE LONG.

Considered to be a truly outstanding example of Georgian architecture in America, Westover *left,* is set in charming, landscaped grounds and was built about 1730 by William Byrd II, the founder of Richmond.

V 21
PRESIDENT TYLER'S HOME

JUST TO THE SOUTH IS SHERWOOD FOREST, WHERE PRESIDENT JOHN TYLER LIVED AFTER HIS RETIREMENT FROM THE PRESIDENCY UNTIL HIS DEATH IN 1862. HE BOUGHT THE PLACE IN 1842 AND CAME TO IT AS HIS HOME IN MARCH, 1845. HERE TYLER, WITH HIS YOUNG SECOND WIFE, ENTERTAINED MUCH AND RAISED ANOTHER LARGE FAMILY. THE HOUSE, WELL-FURNISHED, WAS DAMAGED IN THE WAR PERIOD, 1862-65.

KITTIEWAN AND DOCTOR RICKMAN

TWO MILES SOUTH IS KITTIEWAN, MID-EIGHTEENTH CENTURY MANOR HOUSE. HERE LIVED DOCTOR WILLIAM RICKMAN. FROM 1776 TO 1780 HE WAS DIRECTOR AND CHIEF PHYSICIAN OF THE CONTINENTAL HOSPITALS IN VIRGINIA.

ERECTED BY THE MEDICAL SOCIETY OF VIRGINIA 1977 BY AUTHORITY OF CHARLES CITY COUNTY

Believed to be the oldest three-storey brick house in Virginia, Berkeley *left* was built in 1726 by Benjamin Harrison, a leader in colonial affairs. Two of the mansion's delightfully furnished rooms are shown *on the previous page and below*.

Sited six miles east of Williamsburg, Carter's Grove *above* has been called "the most beautiful house in America". Built in 1750-1753 the impressive building has a 200-foot façade and *right* is shown one of its superbly panelled rooms.

Carter's Grove *these pages*, named by the
famous Robert 'King' Carter, was one of
the plantations that anchored the world of
the Virginia aristocracy and is furnished
with antiques, reproductions and other
furnishings owned by the late Mr and Mrs
Archibald M. McRea, and items from the
Colonial Williamsburg Collection.

The splendid panelled stairway and hall
below left and neighbouring rooms are the
work of the English craftsman Richard
Baylis, who skilfully finished the great suite
of rooms on the river front which has been
described as "the glory of Carter's Grove and
is as fine as any other in the country".

Arranged on two floors are the elegantly
equipped rooms featured *on these pages*
where Thomas Jefferson, George
Washington and other outstanding
Americans of many generations have been
entertained.

Jamestown, the site of the first permanent British settlement in North America, was founded in 1607 with 104 men and boys who had set sail from England on December 20th, 1606, in the tiny fleet of ships, the Susan Constant, Godspeed and Discovery *above left*. Remnants of the old brick buildings *centre left* are preserved in the Colonial Park, where stands the Memorial Church *below left*, erected behind the tower which is all that remains of the first brick church originally constructed in 1639. Created by William Ordway Partridge, the statue *below* is a touching reminder of the daughter of the local chief Powhatan, Pocahontas, a remarkable woman who was to become the wife of the famous John Rolfe. Commemorating the heroic John Smith, without whose leadership the Jamestown colony would almost certainly have foundered, is the massive statue *right and above*, overlooking the broad estuary of the James River, and sculptured by William Couper.

Jamestown Festival Park featured *on these pages*, situated approximately one mile from the site of the original settlement where are preserved the ruins of the old city *below right*, was built in 1957 to celebrate the 350th anniversary of the momentous landing. Here can be seen reconstructions of the forts the settlers built, the huts built by the Indians and the equipment used by the hard-pressed colonists who strove to create a thriving community in spite of the terrible hardships which constantly threatened them. Until the arrival of De La Warr, in June 1610, with more men and supplies, the population, despite reinforcements every year, had been severely decimated by lack of food, disease and overwork. With the introduction of tobacco as a cash crop for export, the achievement of John Rolfe, the community began to prosper and in 1619 the first representative assembly in America was established by Governor Yeardley.

The solitary cannon *below left* is a poignant reminder that it was the Siege of Yorktown which assured the Americans of victory in the War of Independence. Commemorating the hundredth anniversary of the battle is the 95-foot granite shaft of the Victory Monument *above,* the cornerstone of which was laid by President Chester A. Arthur in 1881. Once a bustling seaport, Yorktown still retains some excellent examples of pre-Revolutionary architecture evidenced in the Pate house *centre left,* the town's oldest house *above left* and the Nelson House *right,* at one time the home of Thomas Nelson Jr., Yorktown's signer of the Declaration of Independence. The Courthouse *below,* built in 1955, holds records of York County dating from 1633 and stands on the site which was previously occupied by four earlier buildings.

Contained within a 12-acre park is Richmond's Capitol *below right* and Thomas Crawford's equestrian statue of George Washington *above right* unveiled here in 1858. Built in England 500 years ago and reconstructed in Richmond is the authentic 15th century English manor house, Agecroft Hall *above*. It was at St John's Church *left* that Patrick Henry demanded "Liberty or Death", whilst Hungers Parish Church *below*, on Virginia's Eastern Shore, owns one of the few complete sets of communion silver in existence.

One of the chief exhibition buildings of Colonial Williamsburg, the reconstructed Capitol *above and above left*, is sited at the eastern end of Duke of Gloucester Street. It was here, from 1704 to 1780, that Virginia's General Assembly convened. In the Chamber *centre left* would gather the aristocratic Council, whilst the most important Virginia cases, civil and criminal, were heard in the panelled General Courtroom *below left*.

Typical of many Virginia courthouses is the T-shaped Courthouse of 1770 *below and right*, with its arched windows and octagonal cupola and which stands in the centre of the Market Square.

Dedicated to Sir Walter Ralegh, the many dormered Ralegh Tavern *left and above*, once stood firmly in the foreground of life in the colonial capital. This most famous of Williamsburg hostelries was a centre of social activity – elegant balls were held in its Apollo Room, public receptions were frequent – and it served not only as the business hub, but was also the scene of many public auctions. The reconstructed building follows the design of two wood engravings made by Benson J. Lossing in 1848, whilst the furnishing of its interior *right* was guided by the painstaking inventories of early proprietors.

Jars of medicinal herbs and aromatic spices line the shelves of the apothecary shop *below*.

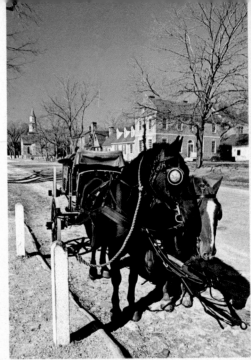

The present Episcopal Bruton Parish Church *below*, with its tranquil interior *above left*, was completed in 1715 and is a fine architectural example of the colonial church in America.

Anthony Hay's Cabinetmaking Shop *above right* was bought by the cabinet-maker in 1756 and today houses two operating craft shops. In the larger wing handcrafted furniture in cherry, walnut and imported mahogany woods is produced and in the smaller section a maker of musical instruments fashions harpsicords and other instruments of the period. The flavour and character of the early colonial days is seen in the clapboard houses and shops with their shuttered windows *centre left, below left and below right*, while the horse-drawn carriage *above* provides an ideal way of touring the historic area.

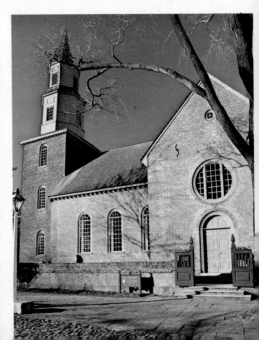

Further examples of the charming clapboard houses are illustrated *on these pages*, including the distinctive red Nicolson Shop *above right*, originally used by Robert Nicolson as both a tailor's shop and store, whilst *below left* is shown a beautifully decorated period carriage.

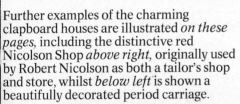

Once the workshop of coachmaker Elkanah Deane, the Deane Forge and Harness-making shop *above* is today occupied by the saddler and blacksmith, whilst in the Gunsmith's Shop *below* exact replicas of the weapons carried by the colonial militia are fashioned and repaired.

The reconstructed King's Arms Tavern *left* is now a public restaurant specialising in traditional southern dishes, and *right* is the Governor's Palace, seen beyond a typical Williamsburg house.

One of Williamsburg's best examples of shop architecture, Prentis Store *left*, was erected in 1740 and occupied for many years by the firm of Prentis & Co. In 1774 when the Yorktown patriots dumped into the York River a shipment of tea in their own "tea-party", it was to this company that the shipment was consigned.

Within the Magazine and Guardhouse *above* is exhibited a collection of 18th century military equipment, including a set of flintlock muskets which were the standard arms of all British and colonial troops.

The impressive cannon *below* stands on the central Market Square, which was an important centre in community life. Restful country greens *above left* are part of Williamsburg's appeal, which is equally as charming in winter, especially when a golden sunset casts its soft glow along the deserted streets *right*.

Below is shown the beautifully tended garden of one of Williamsburg's many restored properties, whilst *above left* can be seen Chownings Tavern, a popular alehouse rebuilt to resemble an 18th century ordinary and operated by the Colonial Williamsburg Foundation. Recognised as an architectural treasure, the Mansion on the historic Shirley Plantation *left* was begun in 1723 by the third Edward Hill and completed in 1770. This magnificent estate has been described as the "oldest and loveliest plantation in Virginia". Sherwood Forest *above*, its beautiful house superbly furnished with family heirlooms of the 18th and 19th centuries, and Berkeley *right*, an ancestral home of two U.S. Presidents, are two of the most splendid of the James River Plantations.

Home of President John Tyler, Sherwood Forest, some 300 feet long, is considered to be the longest frame house in America. Originally built in 1730, the house was renovated and altered during the occupancy of President John Tyler, in 1844, and since that time the working plantation has remained in the hands of the Tyler family. Some of the mansion's elegant rooms are pictured *on these pages* and include: the ballroom, with its arched ceiling and American Empire woodwork *below;* the drawing-room *above;* the main hall *left,* its lovely staircase made of native walnut and pine; the exquisite dining-room *above right* and the delightful Gray Room *right,* President Tyler's family sitting-room.

Built by John Marshall in 1788-1791, the stately house *left,* the only surviving 18th century brick dwelling in Richmond, remained the home of the Chief Justice until his death in 1835. Within the interior *this page* are many original furnishings and family possessions which reveal the simple elegance of this lovely home. Carefully restored as a national landmark, the house is sited on 9th and Marshall Streets.

In 1801 Marshall was appointed Chief Justice of the Supreme Court and for over three decades was responsible for shaping the federal law, succeeding in making the Court an equal authority with those of the Presidency and Congress.

Wilton *top left*, a stately Georgian brick mansion overlooking the James River at Richmond, is today the Museum and Headquarters of the National Society of the Colonial Dames of America. The house is believed to have been built by the leading Williamsburg architect, Richard Taliaferro, between 1750 and 1752, for the third William Randolph. Its handsome interior *above, centre and below left* has panelled walls, primarily in pine, throughout the house, which was restored by Herbert Claiborne.

A modified version of the Pantheon at Rome, the Rotunda of the University of Virginia *below* was created by Thomas Jefferson who devoted himself to the establishment of the University after his retirement from political life. The building, with flanking pavilions which serve as residences for professors, was opened in 1825. Also in Charlottesville is the lovely Castle Hill *right*, whilst *above right* can be seen the Meadow Run Grist Mill and General Store, built in 1797 and which specialises in Virginia handcrafts and antiques.

Begun in 1769, Monticello *these pages*, the beautiful home of Thomas Jefferson, is one of the classic examples of American architecture – its dominating feature the white dome which commands the west front. The three-storey building, comprising thirty-five rooms, is magnificently furnished and includes many of Jefferson's personal mementoes. Today the gardens on the east and west lawns look much as they did during the time of Jefferson's retirement, having been faithfully restored in 1939-40, in accordance with plans which were found among his papers.

Recently renamed Ash Lawn, James Monroe's Albemarle County residence, then known as Highland *above right*, was a simple country home which he affectionately called his "cabin-castle". Although the gardens were not developed until several years after Monroe left the estate, Ash Lawn has become known for its boxwood garden, a focal point of which is the statue of Monroe *below* created by the sculptor Attilio Piccirilli. One of the restored rooms of the house is shown *below left*.

The historic Michie Tavern *above*, now preserved as a museum, contains many genuine furnishings *centre left* which create the original atmosphere of this famous Virginia Tavern of the 1700s. *Below right* is pictured the colourful Keeping Hall, over the mantel of which hangs the flintlock of William Michie, whose initials are carved on the stock, and *above left* the Formal Parlor, converted into a room known as The Ladies' Parlor Bedroom during the occupancy of the Michies.

A fine interpretation of the Georgian style manner, Kenmore in Fredericksburg *above*, home of Colonel Fielding Lewis and Betty Washington Lewis, was built in 1752. The outstanding decorative feature of the house is its plasterwork, seen in the magnificent ceiling of the drawing room *right*, with its exceptionally handsome furnishings, including many authentic examples of 18th century English and American pieces, such as the Chippendale sofa and exquisite cut-glass chandelier.

The Hugh Mercer Apothecary Shop *above left*, with its ancient show-cases, faded prescriptions and gleaming gold-labelled bottles, remains unchanged from those 18th century days when Dr Mercer presided over the drug room. A man of exceptional ability, Hugh Mercer was also a close friend of George Washington, who would come to the doctor's little candle-lit library to discuss, in detail, the impending struggle for independence, for the advice of this talented physician was sought by all. Today this quaint apothecary stands as a Virginia shrine not only to medicine and pharmacy but also to American patriotism. Located in The Chimneys, which was built about 1772 by John Glassell, the Fredericksburg Museum *left* features a variety of exhibits on the colonial period.

Among Fredericksburg's carefully preserved buildings *above* are a wealth of historic houses and museums which are part of the nation's rich colonial heritage. Displayed within the James Monroe Museum and Library *below* are pieces of furniture and possessions acquired by the Monroes during his diplomatic service in France, whilst the interior of the Mary Washington House, featured *above, centre and below left,* is furnished with 18th century pieces similar to those of the period. Pictured *above right* is the impressive Chippendale dining-room of Gunston Hall, the first in the Colonies in the "Chinese taste" and *below right* the kitchen of this handsome residence which was begun by George Mason in 1755.

The construction of Pohick Church, Virginia, was commenced in 1769 according to the plans drawn up by George Washington. Its superb Altar Piece, and pediment window cross, made from walnut from Mount Vernon Estate and covered with gold leaf, can be seen *left*. Preserved in the lovely English country-style Christ Church *below* is the pew of George Washington, whose beloved home, Mount Vernon, is shown *above and overleaf*. Washington's Mill is pictured *right*.

First published in 1979 by Colour Library International Ltd.
© Illustrations: Colour Library International (U.S.A.) Ltd, 163 East 64th Street, New York 10021.
Colour separations by La Cromolito, Milan Italy.
Display and filmsetting by Focus Photoset, London, England.
Printed by NECLOBE, S. A. bound by EUROBINDER - Barcelona - Spain
Published by Crescent Books, a division of Crown Publishers Inc.
Library of Congress Catalogue Card No. 78-74856
CRESCENT 1979

Dep. Legal B. 38.170/1980